How To Get Out of

Job Jail

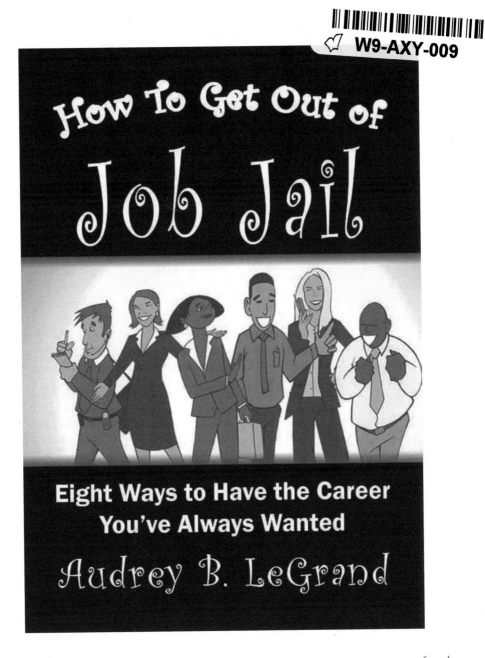

Eight Ways to Have the Career
You've Always Wanted

Audrey B. LeGrand

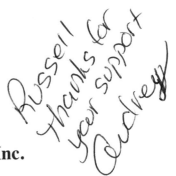

Russell
Thanks for
your support
Audrey

Innovators & Motivators, Inc.
Atlanta, GA

Published in the United States of America by
Innovators & Motivators Inc., Atlanta, Georgia.
ISBN: 0-978-0-615-20171-9 a trade paperback book.

For book orders, author appearance inquiries and interviews, contact the Publisher by mail at:

Innovators & Motivators Inc.
404-534-9393 or email:
audreylegrand@bellsouth.net
www.audreylegrand.com

Library of Congress Cataloging In Publication Data

Acknowledgements

To God be the glory for the things He has done. I thank God for the dream, the team and the means to make this book a reality. I thank God for the 6-year desire to write this book that started with me saying, "No way, I don't have time," or "I don't have anything to say." God turned it around to waking me up at 4:00 am to write out a thought, work on the layout or complete a chapter. An overwhelming desire came over me to finish the book, design the cover and get it published to share with the world.

I thank my earthly father (who has gone to live with my heavenly father), for believing in all my dreams, beginning more than 20 years ago. To my mother, who has supported me every step of the way and still amazes me with her love, devotion, energy and practical-ness at 83 plus years young. I thank you for your unconditional love. To my son, Justin, who is the joy and love of my life, I pray you will be all you can be in life.

To my best friend, Anna, who read every word, revised every word and retyped every word, thanks for your love and patience. I could not have done it without you.

To my special friends: Ben, Kimberly, Lemora, Lois, Marsha and Veronica. You keep me grounded and honest. A special thanks goes to Eddie, my illustrator, for the magnificent job of bringing to life the characters of *How to Get Out of Job Jail.*

And to the reader: I hope on this journey you will see that all things are possible through Christ Jesus who strengthens us. Enjoy the journey to self-discovery and career fulfillment.

Table of Contents

What Happens To People's Dreams?

Unless you are president of your own company, you probably have your eye on a job that is different from the one you have now. If you're a salesperson you might have your eye on the sales manager's position. If you are an accounting clerk perhaps you see yourself as the comptroller for your organization. If you are an assistant buyer, you might dream of heading the purchasing department. It is natural and commendable to have such ambitions. Millions of people aspire to obtain greater heights in their professional lives.

BUT, out of every 100 people with a desire to land a specific job, this is what will happen to each of them over time:

- 55 people will never do anything about it. They will remain stuck in job jail until they die or retire from their current jobs

- 23 will make poor decisions and steer their career in the wrong direction

- 7 will discover that they don't really feel they are entitled to have a better opportunity. Their self-esteem is warped

- 4 will not qualify for a better job. They did not return to school, update their skills or enhance their professional qualities

- 4 will be surpassed by other qualified candidates

- 3 will get better opportunities and subsequently lose them

That leaves just 4 out of every 100 who will get and keep the job they want. There can only be one reason for this grand failure by so many. People simply do not know how to get the opportunities they really want. They set their career goals too high or too low, miscalculating their abilities by under or over estimating them. They refuse to pay the price for adequate educational preparation by not updating their skills and ignore being a life long learner. They spend countless hours spending their energies in a thousand different petty ways that do not relate to their career enhancement.

The rewards for landing a better job are significant. When you're doing what you want to do, you are more productive and you will produce a better quality work. Your superiors and peers recognize your abilities and potential. Your self-confidence increases. You can conquer the world. You begin to acquire new skills because you are eager to learn more. The more you learn, the more you earn. So you set your heights higher and higher. Your personal value to yourself, your family, your employer and your neighborhood/community/world is heightened.

The bottom line is, you will have a good life with enhanced self-esteem, a grand sense of accomplishment, prestige, security and wealth; more than material riches.

Here's the four-step process that will be the running theme throughout this book.

Step 1:
Know your hearts desire!
Make sure you really, really, really want it.

Step 2:
Examine your qualifications

Step 3:
Prepare yourself

Step 4:
Go get it!!!

Introduction

The concept for this book came about as a result of a conversation with a dear friend and fellow trainer. I was a new mother and wanted to work part time. The problem was every part time job I applied for, people felt I was over qualified, that I would become bored and eventually quit.

On the other hand, the positions I applied for were a total career change for me. Companies were reluctant to take a chance on me for fear I would not master the requirements of the new position and ultimately return to my first line of work. I continually received offers for full time employment in the industry where I had previously worked in excess of 65+ hours per week.

At this point in my life, I was not remotely interested in a full time career. None of my three career options were appealing to me. I was over qualified, not interested or not considered for any other category of jobs. Other people were in control of my future. I felt trapped in **Job Jail**.

In sharing my concerns with a friend, she was surprised to find out that she, too, felt trapped in **Job Jail**, for a completely different reason. Her position with a major manufacturer afforded her a very comfortable lifestyle, yet the work itself was not rewarding. She felt as if she did not contribute to the professional or personal growth of any individual she managed. Her position did not influence the bottom line of her organization and she had little opportunity to interact with her firm's clients, customers, suppliers, or vendors.

Yet, with a corner office on the 42nd floor, an administrative assistant at her beck and call, with company perks, it was almost impossible for her to walk away to pursue her passion. She was stuck in **Job Jail** and someone else was controlling her future.

We began to discuss what it would take to gain control of our careers, and to write our own job descriptions. What resulted is a list of nine self-directed career motivators. Here is the list of nine things you have to do while serving time in **Job Jail;** in order to be released, pardoned, or to receive executive clemency from your current line of work.

Nine Step Job Jail Release System

Personal Assessment of your:

1. Communication Skills

    a. Reading

    b. Writing

    c. Verbal

2. Abilities

    a. What have you done in the past?

    b. What do you really enjoy doing now?

    c. What do you want to do in the future?

3. Responsibilities

    a. What skills have you developed in previous positions?

    b. What skills in your past position will help you in future positions?

    c. What skills in your present position will help you in future positions?

Professional Assessment of your:

4. Etiquette Skills

    a. Master the business of good manners

    b. Dress for success

5. Entrepreneurial Skills

    a. Good employees make good career owners

    b. Taking ownership of your career

6. **Enthusiasm**

   a. Get some

   b. Keep some

   c. Give some away

7. **Ethics**

   a. Doing the right thing all the time

   b. The ethics challenge

8. **Relationship Skills**

   a. Recognize what personality types you work best with

   b. Learn how to handle difficult personality types

9. **Self Awareness**

   a. Where are you now and where do you want to be?

   b. What is in your way and how do you feel about what is in your way?

   c. Create some solutions to get where you want to be.

   d. How do you feel about these solutions?

The Time to Start is NOW!

The following work-related questions have been designed to assist you in determining:

- Are you working in a satisfying career that provides you with a good blend of professional rewards and personal pleasure?

- Are you in need of career development coaching in order to take your career to the next level or in a new direction all together?

- Are you trapped in a dead-end job, leading no where but to a life sentence in job jail?

Instructions

Answer each of the following questions yes or no. There is no middle ground for your answers. Answer each question based solely upon your present employment position.

An answer sheet has been provided to assist you in accurately recording and analyzing your responses. The answer sheet is on page 16.

Job Jail Questionnaire

1. Are you more excited about your work than anything else in your life?

2. Would it be easier to remain where you currently are than to look for a new job?

3. Are there days when you accomplish multiple tasks in no time and days when you cannot get a single thing done right?

4. Is your current job a pain, but a necessary step on your career ladder of success?

5. Are you in the right industry, working for the right company, in your ideal position?

6. Do you take work home, work on weekends, on vacation or complete something just before going to bed at night?

7. Is your current position providing a financial base that will allow you to pursue your dream opportunity?

8. Do you have the job or career your spouse, parents, siblings, friends or roommates want you go have?

9. Is your work the topic you prefer to discuss the most?

10. Does the very thought of changing jobs scare you?

11. Do you turn your hobbies or interests into moneymaking ventures?

12. If you take another job and it does not work out, will you be worse off than you are now?

13. Do you take complete and total responsibility for your efforts and productivity outcomes?

14. Do you work more than 40 hours per week on a regular basis?

15. Do you believe it's okay to work more than 40 hours if you enjoy what you are doing?

16. Do you see yourself failing when you try new things?

17. Is your current position a transitional job, which pays the bills while you search for the right opportunity?

18. Are you comfortable where you are?

19. Does your current job allow you to spend the quality time you would like to spend with your family and friends?

20. Do you accomplish your work with enthusiasm and a great deal of energy?

21. Can you quit your current job and not be homeless in less than 3 months?

22. Do you get irritated when people interrupt your workflow?

23. Even when things are going well, do you worry about the future?

24. Are your short-term and/or long-term career goals written down and periodically reviewed?

25. Have your working hours hurt your relationship with family and friends?

26. Are your non-work related activities providing you with professional development opportunities?

27. Do you think about work while driving home or before going to bed?

28. You will not quit your current job because you love it, right?

29. Do you believe more money will solve the other problems in your life?

Answer Key

1. ☐ YES ☐ NO	11. ☐ YES ☐ NO	21. ☐ YES ☐ NO
2. ☐ YES ☐ NO	12. ☐ YES ☐ NO	22. ☐ YES ☐ NO
3. ☐ YES ☐ NO	13. ☐ YES ☐ NO	23. ☐ YES ☐ NO
4. ☐ YES ☐ NO	14. ☐ YES ☐ NO	24. ☐ YES ☐ NO
5. ☐ YES ☐ NO	15. ☐ YES ☐ NO	25. ☐ YES ☐ NO
6. ☐ YES ☐ NO	16. ☐ YES ☐ NO	26. ☐ YES ☐ NO
7. ☐ YES ☐ NO	17. ☐ YES ☐ NO	27. ☐ YES ☐ NO
8. ☐ YES ☐ NO	18. ☐ YES ☐ NO	28. ☐ YES ☐ NO
9. ☐ YES ☐ NO	19. ☐ YES ☐ NO	29. ☐ YES ☐ NO
10. ☐ YES ☐ NO	20. ☐ YES ☐ NO	

How to Total Your Answers

1. Add together all of your yes answers, then add together all of your no answers.

2. Go back through the questions a second time and add together all of your yes answers to even-numbered questions only.

3. Go back through the questions a third time and add together all of your yes answers to odd-numbered questions only.

4. Go back through the questions a fourth time and add together all of your no answers to even-numbered questions only.

5. Go back through the questions a fifth time and add together all of your no answers to odd numbered questions only.

Total number of *Yes* answers   [   ]
Total number of *No* answers   [   ]
Total number of *even Yes* answers   [   ]
Total number of *even No* answers   [   ]
Total number of *odd Yes* answers   [   ]
Total Number of *odd No* answers: [   ]

How to Analyze Your Answers

If your total number of Yes answers is greater than your total number of No answers then your current career is a healthy choice for you and you have a good balance of work and play in your life. Yes answers show a healthy, growing professional involvement in your career management.

If your even-numbered Yes answers are greater than your odd numbered Yes answers, your career choice is okay. Perhaps you should begin to develop a career improvement plan with a professional coach. Even-numbered Yes answers are powered by your enthusiasm for life and the energy you bring to your career.

If your odd-numbered Yes answers are greater than your even-numbered Yes answers, you are headed for Job Jail and a collision course with your conscious about where you really want to be in life. Odd-numbered Yes answers are powered by your fears and driven by your doubt regarding your abilities.

If your total number of No answers are greater than your total number of Yes answers you are serving a life sentence in Job Jail and must begin to ask yourself why are you there? What do you plan to do about it?

Chapter 1 - Communication Skills

No matter what profession or industry you find yourself in, the ability to read, write and speak your logical thoughts will be the single most important interpersonal skill you can develop and consistently rely on throughout your career. Oral and written communication skills rank within the top five skills that all successful professionals posses.

Let's discuss the power of effective communication skills concerning your career advancement.

Communication Skills

In the 21st century, in order for you to advance your career in corporate America, to see a substantial increase in sales, or to obtain additional profits in your own business you must have effective communication skills. You must be a triple threat, able to read, write and speak well. There are no exceptions here. If one of these three areas is holding you back, then the question of the hour is, what do you plan to do about it? Let's examine all three aspects of effective communication skills and the impact each area has on your career mobility.

Reading Ability

As you move forward in your chosen career or continue to build your business, you will find it necessary to have a deeper insight into your industry. You will find yourself reading more trade journals and industry publications in order to find the latest trends, newest information, and the hottest technology for your chosen field.

If you are not currently reading about business trends, management operations, or budget and financing, now would be a good time to get intimate with these terms and procedures. You will need as much information and knowledge about your new chosen field as you can possibly get your hands on. Make it your practice to read everything about your current industry or the new industry you have selected to enter. You must be viewed as a knowledgeable, value-added employee, consultant, or business owner.

You can start by inquiring within your current company library for material or by identifying key personnel within your organization and asking them what industry and business publications they read and what would they recommend you begin to read to advance your career.

Your next step is the internet or your local library for articles relating to trends within your industry or the industry you have selected to go into. Tell your family, friends, and co-workers you would like subscriptions to various industry-related magazines and publications as gifts this year.

Written Communication

Better readers make better writers. Once you begin reading more, your knowledge base will increase and you will find yourself sharing new thoughts, ideas, and procedures with co-workers, peers, managers or your own employees. As you increase your knowledge through reading, your writing ability will improve as well. Your ability to express your thoughts in a written format will expose you to more individuals inside and outside your organization. You will gain new opportunities to present material both orally and in writing (formal/informal) within your organization. Take a business writing class at your local community college to stay abreast of the latest changes.

A better reader, coupled with improved business writing skills increases your exposure to others in your company. People who previously did not know you existed will now have a new attitude regarding your abilities and responsibilities.

With the written word, it is extremely important that all of your documents be proofread for 100% accuracy. The most common mistake writers make in preparing any written document is misspelled words or typos.

You do not have to become a professional proofreader to do an excellent job of catching your own mistakes. Often because we are so familiar with the documents we have written, we do not see the obvious mistakes in front of our faces. This is because psychologically we know what should be on the page. Thoroughly proofing your material will allow you to double check your material.

To proofread thoroughly, it is important to know the most common types of grammatical errors. Professional editors suggest using the following list of errors as your personal checklist when you are proofreading:

- Incorrectly spelled names
- Reversed numbers, in addresses, phone numbers or data
- Incorrect dates
- Incorrect or inconsistent capitalization
- Double typed words or phrases

- Omission of words or parts of words

- Non-agreement of subject and verb

- Misspelled words

Often you may find yourself unable to ask a co-worker or friend to proofread your work. The following tips will assist you in being your own editor/proofreader:

- Always proof read from a printed copy, not from your computer screen. This allows you to see the entire document at once. When you discover a mistake, there will typically be a cluster of errors in nearby sentences.

- Read the document out loud at least twice to make sure it really sounds correct.

- Be on the lookout for commonly misused words, misspelled words or words that sound similar but have different meanings.

- Try to avoid writing and proofreading at the same time. Unless you are under a deadline, put the document down and come back to it. Using a fresh set of eyes on the document is always beneficial.

Typically, you will find spell check on your computer system. This is a wonderful tool that allows you, the writer, to double check your spelling. It can point out misspelled words, find double printed words, identify capital letters at the beginning of a word and suggest when capitalization should be used. However, it does not replace the need for a style guide, a dictionary, a thesaurus, and for proofreading a final copy of your work for grammatical errors. It cannot find typographical errors that appear to be correct, point out grammatical errors or identify poor sentence structure or syntax.

Most of us are not professional proofreaders, nor do we have a desire to become one. However, everyone can learn to more accurately proofread their own writing and catch mistakes before others do. If proofreading becomes a habit for you, your business writing will become more polished and professional.

Verbal Communication

Last but certainly not least, your verbal communication skills must take on a new tone. It is imperative that you demonstrate your ability to effectively connect with a variety of people. We connect best with people by speaking their language. This is easily accomplished by putting forth some effort to understand the way each individual you come in contact with communicates.

This is not as difficult as it sounds. There are four dominant styles of verbal communication with many subsets. The biggest difference in the four styles is the way each communication style takes in information, processes that information and then releases information.

For example, one person may prefer to receive information in writing vs. verbally. Another may ask you to come in person to say what is on your mind.

On the next few pages we will outline each of the four major types of basic communication styles. We will emphasize their strengths, identify their areas of improvement (weaknesses), and detail their preferred method of information delivery.

The Logical /Analytical/Thinker Communicator

This group's central message when they communicate with other people is "do it right." Whatever the project at hand might be, do it right the first time. This communication group is often seen by others as the most serious group of coworkers, family members, or professional peers to interact with. Often thought of as serious thinkers, highly analytical, logical, and rational members of a team they will be easily recognized.

The logical/analytical/thinker communicator is highly organized and loves the details regarding any project or task. They are often considered to be perfectionists and strive to reach it in everything they do, both personally and professionally. They consider it their strength and do not view it as a weakness.

When communicating with the logical/analytical/thinker, remember they want to receive the facts not the fluff about a project. You never have to tell this group how to accomplish something, you only have to tell them why the project, assignment or task should be done. When given a project the logical/analytical/thinker may become bogged down in the details, nitpick and be a little too slow to respond to another person's needs. They may even be critical of others for not taking more time to think, analyze or rationalize the decisions they make in their lives.

The best way to communicate with a logical/analytical/thinker is to be as straightforward as you possibly can, delivering just the facts to them. They prefer to receive their information in writing, so they can read it again and again and think about how they are going to respond. This group of communicators require very little socialization to survive in the work place. They just like to get the job done. They may even pull away or withhold their emotions when stressed.

Review

Central communication theme: *"do it right"*

Strengths: very logical, rational and highly organized, like details and are most concerned with why they are connected to people, places and things. Why is this project, assignment or task being done, is their favorite question. They analyze data and people constantly.

Weaknesses: slow to respond to others because they are still reviewing the facts, analyzing the data and connecting all the dots. They often get too bogged down in the details.

Communication style: prefers to receive information in writing. Allow for lots of white space on the page by using bullet points. When communicating with this group, stick to the facts please.

Percentage of work force population: approximately 35%

The Bold/Controller/Director Communicator

The central message this group of communicators sends out when they communicate with other people is **"get it done."** It does not matter what has to be done, simply get the project done now. The bold/controller/director communicator is often seen by others in the workplace as the most aggressive or most assertive style of communicators. They are often the ones who see the big picture, the bottom-line for their team, before anyone else does.

Truly living up to their central message, they are action and results oriented, fast paced, always on the go, trying to get something accomplished. They make decisions quickly and love a good challenge. They are often the bosses, team leaders, department managers, or unit coordinators. They rally the remaining troops to handle a project. They are the masters of time-management skills because they are usually doing two or more things at once. Their co-workers and colleagues often view them as impatient, straight forward, or misinterpret them as blunt, rude, or sometimes tactless.

It is best to get to the point with the bold/controller/director communicator in concise, tight, bottom-line language. Have your facts ready and get to the point quickly. Do not waste time filling in the picture. If they understand your concept they will get the picture. Their communication preference is for you to put things in writing.

Review

<u>Central communication theme:</u> *"get it done"*

<u>Strengths:</u> take-charge, good leaders, bottom-line people, results and action-oriented people, sees the big picture quickly. Great at rallying the troops quickly to handle a project and enjoys leading.

<u>Weaknesses:</u> very direct and straightforward, possibly blunt and/or tactless at times.

<u>Communication style:</u> prefer information in writing, in concise bottom line language. Gets to the point quickly and supports by facts.

<u>Percentage of work force population:</u> approximately 20%

The Amicable/Supportive/Relater Communicator

This group's central message when they communicate with other individuals is **"let's be friends."** They want everyone in the workplace to get along and be buddies. They are often viewed by the other groups of communicators as friendly, passive, doormats, and pushovers. These are the very people we like to have on our teams and in our departments, not as leaders necessarily, but as teammates and support personnel.

They are reliable, easy going, supportive and caring. All of this characterizes a really good friend. They are loyal and make good team players because they do not seek the limelight for their contributions or want recognition for a successful project completed on time and within budget. They feel it was their job or duty to do these things.

You will easily know them in the workplace because they avoid confrontation and try to keep the peace between co-workers at all cost. Because this is their main objective, they are often a little too slow to respond to inquiries. They spend a great deal of time analyzing how other people will feel about them or their team.

When communicating with this group, remember to be very nice to them, take some time to get to know them for the person they truly are. The best way to achieve this is person-to-person, with face-to-face social communication.

Review

Central communication theme: *"let's be friends"*

Strengths: reliable, dependable, loyal, supportive, good team players, great confidents, and peacekeepers.

Weaknesses: slightly passive, they avoid confrontation at all cost, too slow to respond. They are concerned with their feelings and others' feelings about people, places, and things.

Communication style: person-to-person, face-to-face communication, you must be willing to get to know them (be their friend) before making a request.

Percentage in the workplace: approximately 35%

The Socializing/Expressive/Activist Communicator

This group of communicators can be quickly and easily identified. Their central communication message to everyone they meet is *"let's have fun."* Without a doubt this is the friendliest group of communicators around. Every day at work is an opportunity to party. The smallest accomplishment can cause this group to create a celebration where they start planning who will bring the food.

You will know them in the workplace because of their out-going, creative, expressive, and very animated style of communication. They tend to speak with their whole body. They use their arms, hands and facial expressions to make their point. The socializing/expressive/activist communicator always knows a lot of people. They are eternal optimists and usually persuasive with their ideas. They will work on you until you see their point of view.

However, they are viewed by others as impulsive and impatient. Whenever the project, assignment or task becomes boring, the socializing/expressive/activist communicator will find a way to turn things into a party. They bore easily and many fellow teammates do not view them as strong finishers for important projects, or as strong closers in sales relationships.

It is easy to communicate with this group. Just be upfront and get to the point, yet do not take yourself too seriously. Spend some time getting to know these individuals well. Invest time in socializing with this group of communicators before making your request known.

Review

<u>Central communication theme</u>: *"let's party"*

<u>Strengths:</u> outgoing, friendly, persuasive, know a lot of people, creative, very optimistic, and animated in their communications.

<u>Weaknesses:</u> bores easily, not strong finishers of projects or closers in business.

<u>Communication style:</u> prefers person-to-person, face-to-face, get to know them.

<u>Percentage in the workplace:</u> approximately 10%

Chapter Review

Candid Career Comments

1. Learn the specifics of your style of communication and use it in every aspect of your life.

2. Become familiar with the general attributes of the 3 remaining communication styles

3. Share with others (personally & professionally) your preferred method of communicating (i.e. in writing: emails or memos; verbally: face to face or voice mail messages) Learn to speak up.

4. Respect and use the preferred method of communication others share with you as their preference in every aspect of your life.

5. Remember when you communicate you only make up 25% of the equation. There's another 75% (the other three groups) you don't control, however, it's important to your career to master.

Notes

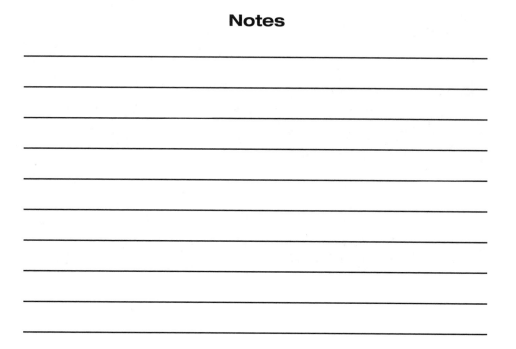

Chapter 2 – Abilities

Often we forget to take inventory of our skills. You must take a daily, weekly, monthly, quarterly, semi-annually, and yearly assessment of your abilities. Remember, this includes your personal and professional abilities.

Do not limit yourself. Ask yourself what are the skills/gifts/talents you most enjoy using? Are you skilled at motivating and leading people, do you prefer to analyze information, or do you prefer to work with your hands creating things?

People skills include mentoring, negotiating, instructing, managing, persuading, serving and/or helping people. Information skills include comparing, copying, complying, computing, analyzing, coordinating and/or synthesizing data. Creative skills include handling, tending to, operating, controlling, setting-up, or precision work.

What do you prefer to do?

As you begin the process of assessing your abilities (determining what you are really capable of doing), begin by asking yourself are you ready, really ready, to make the necessary changes in your career and your life to get you where you want to be in the near future. Start by asking yourself these series of questions:

- Is my career field rapidly changing?
  ☐ Yes   ☐ No

- Is my industry shrinking or growing?
  ☐ Yes   ☐ No

- Am I currently unhappy in my present position?
  ☐ Yes   ☐ No

- Have my career interests changed?
  ☐ Yes   ☐ No

- Have recent personal changes had an impact on my career?
  ☐ Yes   ☐ No

- Has my current position had a negative impact on my health?
  ☐ Yes   ☐ No

- Has my current position had a negative impact on my family, friends, or relationships?
  ☐ Yes   ☐ No

If you find yourself answering yes to two or more of these questions, it is time for you to take serious stock of how and why your current position is having such a negative effect on your life. Remember, it is not what you are called at work that is important but who you are at home that is most important in life.

In order to head in a new direction with a meaningful career a complete and thorough self-analysis must be done. An analysis that includes examining your skills and interests. Ultimately, what you want to understand is how your skills and interests can be utilized in the current marketplace in a meaningful way, therefore, identifying and creating workplace opportunities.

The objective here is to take your interests, coupled with your skills and identify meaningful employment opportunities.

Start by asking yourself, the following questions and taking the time to carefully answer each question:

Step 1

Who are you?

_____

_____

_____

What are you doing for a living right now?

_____

_____

_____

What is it you want to do from now until the end of time?

_____

_____

_____

What would you do, even if you were not paid for it?

_____

_____

_____

What is the difference between what you are doing right now and what it is you want to do?

_____

_____

_____

Step 2

Answer the following questions about your current industry:
What is happening in your current industry?

_____

_____

_____

How is your current industry changing?

_____

_____

_____

Are you prepared educationally and skill-wise to compete in your industry?

_____

_____

_____

Step 3

On the chart on the ***following page***, work on one column at a time and indicate the following information:

- In the first column what skills (tangible or intangible) do you currently possess in each of these areas?

- In the second column indicate how much experience you have in each skill area you identified in column one.

- In the third column you will determine what your skill level is for the skill you identified in column one using the following chart:

  E = Expert
  You can teach someone else the skill

  A = Adequate
  You can perform the skill well

  N = Needs Work
  You can do it but you need to work on improving it

  D = Development
  You do not currently have the skill. You must develop a basic understanding or proficiency.

- In the fourth column identify the skills you will need to master and transition into your new career. Use the chart on the following page.

Skill Category	Years / Months of Experience	Skill Level	Transitioning to a New Career
Operations			
Information Technology [I T]			
Sales / Marketing			
Administrative / Customer Service			
General Management			
Finance & Accounting			
Research & Engineering			
Human Resources			
Other Fields			

What types of jobs are you interested in?

Now that you are armed with this new information and you see a pattern of where your skills, expertise and interest form an alliance, it is time to begin investigating new career options. The first step is to explore the educational and experience requirements of the new field that holds your interest. Next, you must match your talents, skills, and interests to an employer's needs.

This table also becomes a great measuring tool to evaluate potential career offers employers will ultimately make to you. This table will assist you in determining the best fit for yourself. Does the new career have challenging and rewarding opportunities? What is it worth to you now and in the future? Does this position fit your lifestyle? All these questions and more can be answered if you take the time to thoroughly complete this chart.

Step 4

As you continue down this road of self-analysis and career discovery, begin to ask yourself what is it you really want to do in your next career position and make sure you can answer the following questions?

- What responsibilities are you looking for in a new career?

- What task or job functions naturally interest you?

- What type of work environment best suits you?

- Describe a good manager for you to work with?

- Describe the size of an organization that best supports your talents?

- How well do you work under pressure?

- Do you prefer to work alone or on a team?

- Do you enjoy being a member of the team or the team leader?

- Do you define your work or does your work define you?

- Do you prefer external/public contact or internal/employee contact or a combination of both?

- Name the top five things you like most about your current profession?

- How do you respond to authority and power?

- How can you make a significant contribution to an organization?

Step 5

Now that you have successfully answered questions about your current and your new career choice, it's time to turn your attention to your lifestyle and how a new career will fit into your life. Begin to ask yourself the following series of questions:

What type of work environment is best for you?
☐ Formal   ☐ Informal   ☐ Team   ☐ Independent
☐ Offices   ☐ Cubicles   ☐ Open Pits

What type of working hours appeal to you?
☐ Full time   ☐ Part time   ☐ Overtime   ☐ Flex Time
☐ Shift Work   ☐ Weekends   ☐ Irregular Hours

What about the commute to work?
☐ Close to home   ☐ Distance does not matter

How far are you willing to drive? _____

How long are you willing to commute? _____

Is traffic a factor in your decision? ☐ Yes   ☐ No

In your new career choice can you telecommute? ☐ Yes   ☐ No

Is two weeks of vacation enough for you? ☐ Yes   ☐ No

What about the job perks?

_____

_____

_____

What holidays are you looking for that your new employer may **not** be willing to give you off?

_____

_____

How is personal time accumulated and allowed to be used?

_____

_____

_____

Where is your current position taking you?

_____

_____

_____

Are you enjoying the ride?

_____

_____

What changes can you make to secure your present position?

_____

_____

_____

What has been your most rewarding professional accomplishments?

_____

_____

_____

Write down the number of jobs you have had as an adult?

_____

_____

_____

What are the reasons you left each position and the subsequent reason you accepted each new opportunity?

_____

_____

_____

What does this pattern begin to tell you about yourself, your career choices and your work habits?

_____

_____

Where do you want to use these skills?

_____

_____

_____

What are your fields of fascination that can benefit from your talent?

_____

_____

What types of organizations can use your talents?

_____

_____

What needs do these organizations have that you can provide solutions for?

_____

_____

_____

Fill in the blanks on the following statements.

1) I want to work with/for _____.

2) I want to work with/for _____
in the _____area.

3) I want to work with/for _____ in
the _____area
with less than but no more than _____ employees.

Chapter Review

Awesome Ability Analyzers

1. Determine what you are really good at.

2. Identify your areas of improvement (weaknesses).

3. Determine how you will use the abilities you are good at to move into the next phases of your career. Improve your current career, or build your entrepreneurial skills.

4. Create a strategy to start working on your areas of improvement (weaknesses) so you will be able to incorporate those abilities into future career growth.

5. Answer this question: Will your current abilities get you where you want to go or do you need to sharpen your saw, as Dr. Stephen Covey would say in the **7 Habits of Highly Effective People.**

Notes

Chapter 3 – Responsibilities

Now let's talk about what you have actually done in your professional life. What accomplishments and skills can be placed on your resume?

Without looking at your job description start making a list of tasks, assignments, projects, chores, and responsibilities you have had during the life of your career. Span all the way back to your first paying job.

Begin the list today and date it. Work to add things you may have forgotten over the next 10 days, then read over any copies of job descriptions you may have access to and add additional responsibilities over the next 20-day period. After 30 days, you will have produced a complete and thorough list of job responsibilities.

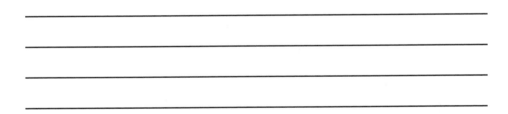

As you continue to take steps towards your new career, consider next the impact your resume will have on prospective employers as you begin your job search. Your resume is a written account of your professional accomplishments. It is not your autobiography. A resume is not the chronological history of your life; rather it should be a representation of your professional accomplishments and experiences.

The three biggest complaints decision-makers have regarding resumes from prospective new hires are:

1. Resumes tend to be poorly organized and prepared.

2. People become so creative in their attempt to be noticed that their resume becomes distracting in its appearance.

3. Resumes are usually too long.

There seems to exist three major misconceptions on the part of candidates regarding what a resume will or will not do for them in their job search.

Misconceptions	Truths
You will need a resume to get a job.	You will need a resume to get an interview. Resumes are door openers. They simply start the interviewing process for most employers. They do not land jobs.
Job offers come by networking, why do I need a resume?	After an initial lead has been derived from a networking contact, a well-written resume presented by you or your contact shows your organizational skills, writing ability, creativity and analytical skills at a glance. It should create enough interest to warrant a phone call for an interview.
Let a prospective employer know everything.	A multiple page resume is a turn-off. The decision-maker will wonder if you can get to the point with your work. If your resume is too short a decision-maker might start to wonder if you regularly overlook details in your work.

So now you are wondering what is right. The length of your resume will be determined by how well you organize and write your professional accomplishments along with telling your professional story. Remember, different audiences prefer different information; so creating two or even three different resumes is very commonplace for today's professional.

All well-crafted resumes should accomplish four things:

1. Assist you in inventorying and categorizing your strengths and weaknesses to determine which accomplishments present you in the best light.

2. It is a calling card, written well enough to get you an interview and assist your network in identifying opportunities for you.

3. It is an agenda for an interview. The decision-maker and you have an outline (a place to begin the journey), during the interview. In the interview is where you breathe life into the resume.

4. It is a memory jogger. Many firms will hold onto resumes from their top candidates for other opportunities.

Resumes have three major components. Think back to your junior high school English class for a moment. A well-written paper has form, style and content. In this chapter we will address each one of these areas separately.

Form

The basics are 8 ½ x 11", 24 pound, 100% cotton or better, ivory, white or gray paper. Black ink looks best on these colors. Use fun colors or odd size paper only if you are a graphics artist, in advertising, marketing, or sales.

The contents can be justified or right ragged, either form is acceptable. However, right ragged is easier for the eye to read. Use a one-inch margin all the way around, using single spacing with larger separations between sections, and bold print for major headings is acceptable.

Style

You have three choices from which to select. Your decision should be based upon the way your individual information presents itself in each of the three styles. Select the one that will put you in the best possible light. Remember your resume is *you* on paper and *you* are unique and special in your work experiences. Your resume does not have to look like anyone else's.

Chronological Resumes

List your experiences in terms of where and when you worked for an organization in reverse order. This is the most well known and the easiest style to compile. It is also effective. Recruiters, employers and decision makers can quickly glance at your accomplishments and determine if you should advance further in the hiring process. The chronological style also works well if you have been on a single career path with progressive growth and you would prefer to stay in the same field. This is a great way to show job maturity, task mastery, and professional growth. The emphasis in the chronological resume is on where you have been employed.

Functional Resumes

Include a listing of your professional experiences in clusters under major skill headings. If you have strong communication skills, under this heading you would list a variety of supporting experiences, which you obtained from different jobs, school, or volunteer situations. A functional resume requires great thought and planning. You will need to spend time organizing your experiences by specific skills and then determine how these skills will be listed on your resume, followed by where you obtained them. This format is great for career changers and the upwardly mobile, fast tracker. Often candidates prepare two or three different functional resumes, because each one highlights a different set of professional skills.

Chronofunctional Resumes

Is a combination of the previous two styles. This style is for movers and shakers. You will need a strong summary statement, followed by descriptions of your functional skills, followed by the company names you have worked for. You will repeat these steps for each employer you decide to use.

Content

This will require some thought and good planning. Think about what you did on a daily basis as well as your major accomplishments over time. These achievements will then become powerful statements that will give your resume the extra get up and go it needs to stand out in a sea of resumes.

Here is an easy way for you to think about your accomplishment statements. Use the acronym C.A.R.S. They take us from one place to another and people tend to drive them fast. The same principle applies to your career. You want your career to be on the move.

C = Career accomplishments or Challenges in the workplace

What challenges, problems, or objectives were you responsible for on a daily weekly or monthly basis? These challenges gave you an opportunity to create some solutions for your company. Thereby showing your initiative, critical thinking ability, creativeness, and willingness to resolve problems, or streamline a process. Each solution handled with professionalism, became a career accomplishment to be proud of. Think of accomplishments and challenges you had in your career.

A = Action [what you actually did]

Think about the physical action you took to achieve the accomplishment or to meet the challenge. In detail explain what you did in regards to each accomplishment or challenge placed before you. This statement always starts with an action verb. (See the partial listing at the end of the chapter for examples of action verbs).

R = Results

When you took physical action you created a reaction and obtained favorable results. Now it is time to share the results of what you accomplished with a prospective employer. Your results should be expressed in quantifiable or numerical terms, such as dollars and cents, percentages, an increase or decrease of something, (i.e. time, volume, revenue, profit, morale, etc.).

S = Scope

When you dealt with the challenges presented to you, you took a course of action which produced results. All of these activities collectively had an impact on your company. Now, think about who was affected by your actions, and the results produced.

Example 1:

Challenge was: several accidents and workplace injuries had occurred in the last 6 months. It was difficult to pinpoint the various causes.

Action taken: initiated an employee survey on workplace safety procedures to determine areas of vulnerability. Ascertained the current level of employee knowledge regarding the correct way to report incidents.

Results: implemented new safety procedures reducing workplace accidents by 25% over a 3-month period.

Scope: affected all 1,000 company employees.

The Complete Accomplishment Results Statement would be:

Initiated an employee survey that resulted in the implementation of new safety procedures reducing workplace accidents by 25% over a 3-month period affecting all 1,000 plant employees.

This statement can be used on a resume to demonstrate to a prospective employer precisely what you have accomplished in your previous position and the skills you demonstrated to achieve this accomplishment. Remember, you are thinking of the small parts before you see the whole picture.

Example 2:

Challenge was: extensive delays in processing invoices for reimbursement of expenses created a backlog of invoices to be paid.

Action taken: reorganized and streamlined accounting and vendor payment procedures.

Results: a $150,000 annual savings to the company in accounting expenses.

Scope: eliminated the overtime worked by the 12 member team in the accounting department.

The Complete Accomplishment Results Statement would be:

Reorganized and streamlined current accounting and vendor payment procedures for the 12-member accounting department. Yielded an annual savings of $150,000 to the company which decreased turn-around time for vendor payments and eliminated the need for overtime hours.

Exercise: Create some get up and go for your resume using the C.A.R.S. acronym.

Challenge + **A**ction + **R**esults + **S**cope = Career Accomplishment Statement for my resume.

C = Challenge

_____

_____

_____

A = Action

_____

_____

_____

R = Results obtained

_____

_____

_____

S = Scope

_____

_____

_____

Career Accomplishment Statement

_____

_____

_____

More C.A.R.S. Worksheets can be found in the Appendix.

Notice that more lines were provided for the action taken section of this exercise than the other sections. Concentrate your thoughts in this area and remember exactly what appears on your resume will start with the action verbs you select in step 2 and end with the scope or impact on the organization in step 4.

Rule of Thumb:

Create 15-20 career achievement result statements and use 6-10 of them on any one resume. Use the remaining statements on a second or possibly third resume. Group the statements together by job and task related functions. This depends on how long and strong each statement is and how much space is available. I strongly recommend that you create 20 or more career achievement statements, group them together by functions, and select different ones to appear on different resumes.

Action Words

This is just a small sample list of action words to stimulate your thinking as you begin to prepare your C.A.R.S. statements.

Administered	Expanded	Planned
Analyzed	Implemented	Presented
Controlled	Improved	Promoted
Coordinated	Increased	Reduced
Created	Initiated	Reviewed
Designed	Innovated	Researched
Developed	Instructed	Scheduled
Diagnosed	Integrated	Solved
Directed	Modified	Supervised
Eliminated	Negotiated	Trained
Established	Organized	Troubleshooted

Chapter Review

Rev Up Your Remarkable Responsibilities

1. Decide if what you have been responsible for in the past is what you want to be responsible for in the future.

2. Learn to follow you passion vs. pursuing your pension.

3. Determine the level of responsibility you want to have in your new opportunity (i.e. entry level, expert, or decision making).

4. Identify which responsibilities you do not want to have in your next opportunity (i.e. cleaning the break room, lead surgeon).

5. Create a strategy to use your best abilities and current responsibilities to chart a new career path.

Notes

Chapter 4 – Business Etiquette

Ellen is busy mastering the basics of better business etiquette. Business etiquette is often overlooked as no longer being a necessary courtesy in today's hectic and competitive business world. However, research shows that the basic common courtesies our mothers taught us, before sending us off to school, still serve us well in the business world.

In this chapter, we will discuss mastering the basics on good business etiquette in order to advance your career. In order to be considered a true professional you must master three key elements to good business etiquette. They are:

1) Manners – how you show kindness and consideration to others

2) Etiquette skills – rules of behavior in our society

3) Leadership skills – setting a positive example for others by doing the right thing, at the right time, all the time

Savvy professionals take the business of good manners very seriously. It can be the difference between a rising star who is on the fast track, or an employee who cannot even start the engine on his/her career. The star employee masters the little nuances of business etiquette that others have not. Those are the subtle differences that can impress a potential client, influence a decision maker, or make or break a meeting/interview.

In this chapter, we will explore the three concepts and show you ways to improve your manners, business etiquette, and leadership skills. Most people think of etiquette in its traditional sense, i.e., which fork goes to use; how to set a formal table; how to send or respond to an invitation, etc. Business etiquette is so much more. It is how we contribute to a healthy team environment, how we respond to a racial or sexually insensitive joke, how we interact with senior management, or how we deliver unpleasant news to a customer.

Barbara Jordan once said, "If you're going to play the game properly, you'd better know every rule." Often in our careers, we are faced with playing a new game and we have no rule book, or the rules change and no one tells us.

Let's start with the basics of formal business introductions. They need to be addressed. As professionals, this is a skill we all must master.

When meeting someone you do not know, stand up, smile, extend your right hand and say,

1. "Hello, my name is _____."
   Your response to an introduction is
   "It's nice to meet you {insert their name here}.

   OR

2. "It's a pleasure to meet you {insert their name here}.
   My name is _____."

Introduction Rules

There are a few introduction rules that should always be followed.

1. Introducing a man to a woman - the woman's name is always stated first.

   Example: Renee Smith, I would like you to meet Ben Bridges. Ben Bridges this is Renee Smith.

2. Introducing an older person to a younger person - always state the older person's name first.

   Example: Mrs. Jones or (Eva Jones) I would like to introduce you to Anna Wilson. Anna Wilson this is Mrs. Jones or (Eva Jones)

3. Introducing a person of importance - always state the important person's name first.

   Example: Judge Ellis or (Judge Walter Ellis) this is Lois Price. Lois Price this is Judge Ellis or (Judge Walter Ellis).

Shaking Hands

Why do we shake hands in our society? When you are introduced, extending your hand for the initial handshake expresses respect, consideration and friendliness. It simply shows how pleased you are to meet that person.

When do we shake hands? When you meet someone new and when someone extends their hand to you, you must offer your hand back. It is rude to ignore an extended hand. These are the two instances where good manners should always be applied. Any other time you wish to shake hands is your choice.

When do we not shake hands? When someone's hands are full and they will be unable to extend their hand or when meeting a physically challenged individual (i.e. arthritis or prosthesis).

Let's talk about how to shake hands. The proper way is to extend your right hand (never your left), and clasp the other party's right hand firmly. In our culture, we use the web-to-web approach when shaking hands. The web of your hand is the space between your thumb and forefinger. This area should connect with the other person's web for a proper handshake.

The next thing to consider is the amount of firmness to apply. We are either guilty of being too weak or too firm. Gripping someone's hand with the right amount of firmness may take some time to master. Practice does make perfect in this instance. Remember there are people in our society who are sensitive about extending their hands, (surgeons, hand models, artists, musicians, etc.) for fear of injuring their hands and upsetting their means of making a living.

In addition to the right amount of firmness, you must become comfortable with looking directly into the other person's eyes and maintaining good eye contact. Eye contact is a way of showing respect. In addition, remember to smile after all, this is supposed to be a friendly gesture. You are glad to meet this new person... aren't you?

Rules for shaking hands

1) A woman offers her hand to a man first.

2) An elderly person offers to shake a younger person's hand.

3) A person of significance (someone holding a title, office) extends their hand first.

4) Physically challenged (their right arm is impaired). You should simply touch their upper right arm/shoulder area as a sign of a greeting. Everything else remains the same.

Do not stare at their disability and do not ask personal questions during the introduction. This is the beginning of a business relationship that could produce a friendship as well. You will have enough time to get to know the individual. Kindness and consideration provide the basis for all good manners. Exercise good manners whenever you are meeting someone new.

Leaving Voice Mail Messages

There seems to be one thing many of us are guilty of when leaving a voice mail message. The message is too long and our call back number gets eliminated or rushed through at the end of the message. Let's reverse the process and our line of thinking so when you're leaving a voice mail message you start with your name, then phone number next, so it is at the beginning of the message and stated slowly and clearly. This will enable the listener to write the number down correctly the first time.

There are five key elements to a good voice mail message:

1) State who you are

2) Slowly and clearly leave your call back number

3) State your message (concise and brief)

4) State the best time to return your call

5) Leave the day and time of your call

Example: Sandra, this is Jimmy at extension 1024. I wanted to know if you could have the Allen report ready for courier pickup at 5:00 pm today. It's Wednesday morning around 11:00 am and I will be in my office all day if you need to reach me. Thanks. Most of us leave our phone number last and rush through the number.

Email Messages

Cyberspace has created its own unique set of rules called "netiquette" to govern the way people interact with one another on the internet. There are two which hold the most significance for good business etiquette. They are the techniques of shouting and spamming when it comes to email.

You may have a point to prove and a message to convey but you can express it well without using all capital letters in an email message. This is considered rude "netiquette." Everywhere else capital letters are just that - capital letters, but on the internet they are viewed as a rude and offensive way of communicating your point. Email messages are letters so remember the rules of composition from 7th grade still apply to this easy and convenient form of communication. Want to impress someone in an email message, set your email up to look just like a standard business letter.

Spamming is the cyberspace term for mass mailing of commercial advertisements whose origins are difficult to trace. Just like the mystery meat, Spam, keep in mind when you cross-reference similar material to numerous email groups, you could be considered a spammer.

Spamming is viewed in cyberspace as junk mail and unnecessary. It is also viewed as rude and extremely poor netiquette, because it always seems to grow. People frequently reply to the unwanted, unsolicited email messages by hitting the reply to all bottom and now everyone who received the first useless email message now receives your reply. It just creates its own life cycle. Avoid all mass mailings. You do not have permission to use someone's email address to circulate every piece of trivia, inspirational, motivational sayings, or advertisement known to mankind.

Cell Phones

With the introduction of cellular phones, our lives have become more hectic than ever. More of us are now on an electronic leash. We are more accessible and more connected. Cell phones are very useful when used properly.

For instance, you can call ahead to confirm your next appointment or to let someone know you are stuck in traffic, running late, or need better directions. However, they can be annoying in public places such as restaurants, movie theaters, churches, stores, schools, day cares, etc.

Remember two important things for proper phone usage:

1) If you call someone's cell phone keep it brief and to the point.

2) Conversations on cell phones are NOT private and may be legally monitored.

What's your BEIQ? (Business Etiquette Intelligence Quotient)

Demonstrating appropriate behavior in business settings is a sure fire way to show a favorable impression for your organization, build strong relationships and get ahead in your career. In today's highly competitive job market practicing good etiquette and showing common courtesies make even more sense. If you think business etiquette has gone away, just like the manual typewriter, think again.

This easy quiz can be completed in 5 minutes or less and your answers will give you great insight into your etiquette skills.

1. You're in an associate's office, gathering information when his phone rings. It might be him calling you with further instructions, so you answer. It happens to be a client, should you:

   a) Say that Bob is out right now and to call back

   b) Say that Bob is recovering from an injury and will be out of the office for the next several weeks

   c) Tell the client he has reached Bob's office; give your name and the option of leaving a message or calling back later

   d) Take care of the problem yourself without ever identifying yourself

2. You are invited to a business associate's home for dinner. You should:

   a) Bring a dish instead of a gift

   b) Take nothing because business related dinners do not require a gift

   c) Take an expensive gift to make a good impression

   d) Take a small gift

3. You are the host of a small group of business associates, who gathered for dinner. Who should lead the group to the table?

   a) The women in the group

   b) As the hostess you should go first

   c) The highest ranking person in the group goes first

   d) The people in the group go first based upon seniority

4. You are at a business lunch with upper management. The waiter has served you, what do you do?

   a) Begin eating only if others have started

   b) Wait for the women at the table to be served

   c) Begin eating

   d) Wait until everyone is served

5. You knock your beverage glass over at a business luncheon with an important client, what should you do:

   a) Apologize and do whatever you can to clean up the mess

   b) Don't make a fuss, cover the spill with your napkin and call over the waiter the next time you see him.

   c) Blot the spill with your napkin and other people's napkins, if they offer and call the waiter.

   d) Jump up immediately to find the waiter

6. While you're attending a networking function, you see someone who looks vaguely familiar, what should you do:

   a) Ignore her in case she's someone else

   b) Pretend to know her

   c) Ask her if she remembers you

   d) Introduce yourself

7. How should you greet a visitor who just entered your office?

   a) Stand and greet her and offer a chair

   b) Let her choose a seat herself

   c) Lean across the desk and shake hands

   d) Call out a casual greeting and finish your personal task

8. Your cell phone just went off in the middle of a training workshop, what should you do?

   a) Answer the call in a low voice to cause the least possible disturbance

   b) Run outside as quickly as possible to catch the call before it rolls over into voicemail

   c) Glare pointedly at the person sitting next to you until the ring stops

   d) Switch off the phone and apologize quietly to those around you, and return the call during your break

9. You are scheduled to depart on a business trip, the same day an important client has extended an invitation to lunch. What should you do?

   a) RSVP, then cancel at the last minute if your trip comes through

   b) RSVP, so you're covered, then don't go if your trip comes through

   c) Ignore the RSVP because you probably can't attend.

   d) Call the client and explain the situation. Ask if you can RSVP at a later date.

10. A colleague has introduced you to Mr. Bridges. His name tag reads "Ben Bridges," how should you address him?

    a) Ben

    b) Mr. Bridges

    c) Avoid addressing him by name

    d) Ben Bridges

11. The CEO of your company and his wife come to your table at a company holiday party. Both are older than you are. What is the proper way to greet the couple?

    a) Greet the wife first, then the CEO, shaking hands with both

    b) Greet the CEO first, then the wife, shaking hands with both

    c) Greet the wife first, but do not offer to shake hands until she initiates

    d) Greet the CEO first, greet the wife second, no need to shake hands

12. Where should you place the butter you just sliced from the butter dish?

    a) Set the dish beside your plate, take a pat of butter and butter your bread

    b) Put a pat of butter on the side of your bread plate, pass the dish, then apply the butter to your bread

    c) Put a pat of butter on the side of your bread plate, then break off a bite as needed and butter only that small piece

    d) Buttering bread is unsophisticated. Skip the butter

13. What is an appropriate holiday gift for your largest client?

    a) A gift basket of expensive liqueurs

    b) A gold watch with the company logo engraved on it

    c) A $100 gift voucher for the company store

    d) A $100 gift voucher to an exclusive men's or women's accessories store

14. Terry has a new boss, what would be an appropriate gift for her for the holidays?

    a) A funny poster, framed for her office

    b) An expensive bottle of liquor

    c) A subscription to a magazine

    d) A good quality pen

15. You are at a professional networking event. In the small group you where are standing, you know everyone. But the other members of the group do not know each other. You have drawn a blank on one person's last name. What should you do?

    a) Pretend you think they all know each other

    b) Apologize and ask for his name

    c) Ask everyone to introduce themselves

    d) Make a big deal about your memory loss

Chapter Review

Exercising Eloquent Etiquette

1. Apply the sundown rule to your professional life. If you get a call or email today, acknowledge it, even if you have to buy yourself time to accurately research and respond to the caller's request.

2. Always have a professional voice mail message that contains your name, phone number and a pleasant message.

3. A formal R.S.V.P. is a notice that the host or hostess requests a response indicating whether an invited guest will attend the function. Remember a reply is mandatory as soon as the invitation is received to allow the host/hostess to make plans.

4. A firm, not tight, or wimpy handshake is the accepted greeting in our American culture. Hugging and kissing is not acceptable, even between two consenting adults during business hours. Individuals, who due to health reasons, disability, or neurosis cannot shake hands should offer their guest a brief but courteous explanation.

Answers to etiquette questions

1. C	2. D	3. B
4. D	5. B	6. D
7. A	8. D	9. D
10. B	11. A	12. C
13. B	14. D	15. B

Scoring:

12-15   Excellent - You have excellent etiquette skills, keep up the great work

8-11   Good – Your etiquette skills are good, so just work on the specific areas where you need to get better

8 or below   Help – You are in need of a good etiquette class and/or business coach to help you refine tour social skills

Notes

Chapter 5 – Entrepreneurial Skills

Ellen is busy multi-tasking; a skill so many of us have mastered or we are in need of tackling right away. As you examine your career, begin to notice that the same skills successful entrepreneurs possess are often the exact skills good employees exemplify. In this chapter we will explore how becoming an employee with entrepreneurial skills can help you advance your career. You could remain in your current career but establish your own business within the organization. Conversely, you could employ entrepreneurial skills and over time with effective planning become a true entrepreneur, managing and operating your own business.

When we think of entrepreneurship, we often think of individuals owning and operating their own small business. Usually small businesses grow over time to be mainstays in our local economy. However, let us not limit our perception of entrepreneurship to strictly business owners. The very same skills used by successful entrepreneurs are the skills used by successful employees everyday.

Time Management	Sensitivity Skills
Effective Communication Skills	Coaching Skills
Multitasking	Persuasion Skills
Mastery of Your Subject Matter	Evaluation & Assessment Skills
Organizational Skills	Analytical Abilities
Project Management	Good Writing Skills
Presentation Skills	Communication Skills

For example, think of yourself as a business, ME, Inc.; define your product, the service(s) you will provide or your area of expertise. Every business must know its target market. Decide on an individual basis to whom you are going to sell your product, provide your services to and/or make your expertise and knowledge available to.

A good entrepreneurial-employee answers the following question many times. Why does everyone come to me? A good entrepreneurial-employee understands why their customers buy from them, why clients request their services or pay for their knowledge.

A good entrepreneurial-employee is driven to success by the quality of the product provided, the service they deliver, or the benefits of the advice given. The hallmark of your business should be ultimate customer satisfaction. In order to provide outstanding customer service you must know what is going on in your industry, what are the latest trends, growth potential, or if the industry is becoming obsolete.

All good entrepreneurial-employees invest in their own personal growth and career development the same way successful companies invest in research and development. Ask any entrepreneur what they will be able to provide? The entrepreneur will be on top of the latest trends in their industry and know where they are positioning themselves.

An entrepreneurial-employee must be flexible enough to consider changing various aspects of their business. Over time you may need to start from the ground floor again. You keep abreast of how globalization will affect your career, business, industry, etc. You will increase your individual value to the organization by understanding and being able to articulate globalization implications on your workload, business and/or industry.

All good entrepreneurial-employees stay alert to the possibilities of mergers and acquisitions. You may find yourself competing for your job with a co-worker or employee from the acquired organization. Are you prepared to compete for business opportunities?

Are you a good employee? If so, then you could be a good entrepreneur. The choice is yours. To assist you in making these choices, consider your responses to the following questions:

Do you work well alone?   [ ] Yes   [ ] No

Does your competitive drive come naturally?   [ ] Yes   [ ] No

Are you confident?   [ ] Yes   [ ] No

Can you make tough decisions quickly and live with
the results of those decisions?   [ ] Yes   [ ] No

Do you try even harder after being told,
"No, it can't be done?"   [ ] Yes   [ ] No

Are you always thinking of ways to improve
something or yourself?   [ ] Yes   [ ] No

Can you display a positive outlook even
during a hectic day?   [ ] Yes   [ ] No

Do you possess the drive to succeed no matter what?   [ ] Yes   [ ] No

If you answered **yes** to 6 or more of these statements, you are the kind of employee that would also make a good entrepreneur.

Chapter Review

Extraordinary Effective Entrepreneurship

1. When times are tough you can't afford to wait for someone to provide you with a job. You have to create your own by identifying a need and developing the skills to fulfill that need.

2. Fear keeps us from taking action and if we don't act, we never get beyond where we are now.

3. The tragedy in life does not lie in not reaching your goals. The tragedy lies in not having goals to reach.

4. Every time I fail, I know I am that much closer to the success I want.

5. Seek the advice and cooperation from those around you but never seek their permission to pursue your dreams.

Excerpts from *Motivational Moments for Entrepreneurs*, complied by Audrey B. LeGrand.

Notes

Chapter 6 - Enthusiasm

There will be good days and there will be dark days along this journey. However, you must not give up on your career pursuits. Where will you be if you give up?

Seek out and deliberately find other like-minded individuals to be a part of your support group but more importantly, a part of your accountability club. You will need people to motivate you and move you to newer and higher heights.

Read and consume only motivating, inspiring, upbeat, and positive material. Surround yourself with positive reminders that your best is yet to come. You are solely responsible for making it happen with constant planning and persistent work. Today is a new day and a great time to begin your career with great enthusiasm!

The ABC's of Enthusiasm

A is for attitude

Your **attitude** is your altitude. How you view yourself, the work you do, how you interact with others, the value you place on your work ... all play into how you react to situations, places, things, and people. If you are positive, optimistic, open and receptive to what happens to you, you can always find the value or lesson in every experience you have.

On the other hand, if you are negative, pessimistic and bitter you will see the world and your experiences through a very narrow outlook. You will actually shorten your life span.

B is for better, best and be bold

While you concentrate on getting **better**, offer the world your very best everyday. At the end of the day, did you give it your all? If you did, assess what went right for you today and repeat those actions as often as you can.

If after your daily assessment you identify things that can be done differently or better, next time strive for that. There is nothing you can do to change the past; you can only work to make the future better.

C is for creativity and challenges

Use your **creativity** each day. Unleash your creative energies in new and different directions. Thinking outside the box means when you see something that is not in your realm of reality (your box), you have two choices, increase the size of your box so that it includes this new idea. Then, reach outside the box and embrace the idea, and make it happen.

We each have to make serious choices in our lives. Choices that will result in major changes as we face various challenges. We can always be prepared to make wise choices, implement changes, and handle the challenges of life, with God's help.

D is for determination and dedication

Once you have identified what it is you want, be **determined** to make it happen. Do not settle for talking about it. Let nothing and no one get in your way. Look for ways to solicit help and get people to assist you. If not, you will have to use your creativity and imagination to design ways to go around, under, or over your obstacles. This will show others your determination to make things happen and your dedication to your ideas and plans.

E is for enthusiasm and exploration

Allow your passion and **enthusiasm** for all your projects to shine through in everything you do. That enthusiasm or love will allow you to **explore** the unknown without fear. This enthusiasm will become your driving force. Many things and people may try to get in your way so seek encouragement from motivational readings, and people, as well as your faith. Never operate on an empty tank. Always fill your spirit and mind with positive things and then allow those positive things to show through in your enthusiasm.

F is for fearless and feedback

"There is nothing to **fear** but fear itself." We are born with only two innate fears. They are the fear of heights or falling and the fear of loud noises. If you are afraid of anything else you have been taught or conditioned over time to be afraid. In order to pursue your life's passion you will have to be fearless, never ending, never stopping, or settling for less than what you desire. Develop a fearless attitude regarding everything you do.

As you travel this path to success ask for constructive **feedback**. People will come into your life for a reason and a season. Identify their reason early on in your relationship and that will help you determine their season. Always ask for specific feedback from the people in your life about what you are doing and plan on doing.

G is for greatness

There is a place on earth that is filled with untapped potential. Do you know where it is? Answer: the cemetery. People die everyday without discovering or using any of their God given talents. Do not allow this to happen to you. Explore your full potential and put it to good use, first in small ways to make a difference in your life, your family, your workplace, then your place of worship, and your community. Do not be ashamed to display your *greatness* in random acts of kindness. Make it a habit to do something good for someone else everyday.

H is for hard work

What you have elected to do will be *hard* work. No doubt about it. But plan your work and work your plan. Make small strides toward your personal or professional goals. Afterward, the bigger picture does not look so daunting. The journey of 1,000 miles begins with the first step. Hard work builds character and strength. Hard work will lead you to your heart's work.

I is for introspective

On a weekly basis, take an introspective (internal) look at who you are and where you are going. Ask yourself this question, is the person I am right now the person I want to live with for the rest of my life? If you answered *yes*, you are happy with your personal, professional and spiritual life. If you answered *no*, you have work to do in one or more areas.

J is for judgment

Reserve passing your personal *judgment* on situations and people until you have walked in their shoes. Never be too critical of someone's decisions until you have all the facts. This is a difficult one for most of us to master. So here's an area of growth and an opportunity for all of us to learn to listen more and speak less.

K is for knowledge

Acquire as much *knowledge*/information as you possibly can about your areas of interest. You must learn more each year to earn more. What new skills have you acquired? What new skills do you plan to add to your tool belt this year?

L is for leadership and loyalty

"To thine own self be true." Be *loyal* to yourself first and then to others. Be honest with yourself about where you are and where you want to be. What is the point of fooling yourself? Once you have clearly thought through your goals remain committed to the end and see them to reality.

Leadership skills that display initiative will move you along further in your new career than you can imagine. You will need to take the lead in your life; if there is ever a chance for you to succeed.

M is for meditate

Find some quiet time each day, (3 minutes, 5 minutes or 15 minutes) to calm yourself and reflect on all the good things in your life. God is truly in the blessing business. Each morning we are allowed to open our eyes there is something good about that day. To help you in this endeavor, buy a journal and record your thoughts, prayer requests and praise reports on a daily basis. The victory is in the journey and the journey is your process to fulfillment. Make sure everyday has quiet time in the morning or the evening.

N is for noble

Be *noble* and honest in all your acts of kindness and be considerate to others. Make your word your bond and act accordingly.

O is for optimism

None of us knows enough to be pessimistic about our career outcomes. Remain eternally *optimistic* about everything you do. See the life lesson in every endeavor and frequently ask yourself what is the lesson I am learning here? If you are stuck in a rut you will have to enlarge your box or come out of the box to experience new things. You will never have more than you already have, if you do not try anything new.

Surround yourself with positive people, sayings, and places. Eliminate the negative in all aspects of your life. This does not mean there will not be down days and mistakes made, but you will view them as learning experiences and grow from them. Remember, "as a man thinketh so is he."

P is for pride and preparation

It is far better for a person to be **prepared** and have no opportunity than for a person to have an opportunity and not be prepared. Every small step you take toward your goal brings you one step closer to reaching new realities. Make small progress everyday and reward yourself accordingly.

Take great *pride* in all that you do and say, for it will come back to you. Allow the quality of your words to shine through on all of your undertakings. No more sloppy reports, resumes or company presentations. Take pride and personal ownership in all your endeavors.

Q is for questions

Question: Where do you stand and where are you going everyday? Where are you today? Where will you be next week? What endless possibilities does next month hold for your successful future? It is alright if you change directions on the journey, just start the journey and move ahead. You can write or rewrite the road map as you go. Just get moving.

R is for respect and responsibility

It is time to own up and take *responsibility* for your future. Take responsibility for the outcomes you desire and ask yourself, what must I do to make this happen? Along the way, respect other people's opinions. As you respect others, they will respect you.

S is for strength

You will need great physical strength to run this race. Eat right, exercise and get the proper amount of sleep. See your doctor and dentist and know that everything is okay with your health. Learn to control what might be out of control in your life. You will need lots of stamina to endure the obstacles that will come your way. The more physically fit you become the better mentally fit you will become. You will be able to better respond to good challenges and bad situations.

T is for tenacity

You will need an unshakable will to survive and thrive in hard times if you plan on making it. You must have a burning desire to succeed that supersedes all other desires. This desire has to be almost unexplainable to others. Why would you continue to pursue a career, a degree, a promotion or a business opportunity day after day if it was not for your *tenacity*? Become like a mad dog. Do not allow anyone or anything to turn you around and take your dream from you.

U is for uniqueness

You are special and you have something special inside of you that only you can give to the world. Discover what your *uniqueness* is and give it to the world with a smile. You will feel better and the world will be better as a result of your unique contribution.

V is for value

There is *value* in the valley and value in all experiences. What have you learned that you value from your experiences? You won't see the value if you are still agonizing on the bitterness of the experience. Life's good and bad things happen to us and make us value every experience, for there is a lesson in each experience. We are more than conquers, we are victorious!

W is for Willingness

It is worth the work. Are you **willing** to give it your all? You know it will be worth it in the end. Anything worth having is worth working for. An overnight success takes approximately 15 years to make happen. Are you willing to work that hard continuously and consistently for that amount of time or longer to fulfill your dream? 85% of people talk about what they are planning to do; only 15% actually do what they talk about.

X is for x-ray

Examine people, places, things, situations and challenges with an open mind. Examine everything and everyone that comes into your life. Ask questions until you get answers and determine for yourself if this is someone or something sent to help you or hurt you. People come into our lives for a reason and a season. We never know if the season is short or long or if the reason is good or bad until we examine what people say and do. Examine their motives carefully. My grandmother used to say everything that feels good to you isn't good for you.

Y is for yourself

Shakespeare once said 'to thine own self be true.' This is extremely important in this day and time. We are pulled in so many different directions with work, family, friends, church, etc. Somewhere in all of this you can get lost. Before you know it, someone else or something else has taken over your life and you have lost control of your goals. You have been placed on the back burner. This can be good or bad depending on how you view it. As long as everyone knows this situation is a detour and not a dead-end, some diversion in your game plan can be healthy.

Z is for zeal

Once you have assessed your abilities, clearly identify your interests and begin to actively pursue your goals, you must show your passion for your choices. You must maintain this zeal for life and your interest at all costs. Don't allow anyone or anything to steal your zest for living.

Chapter Review

Exciting Enthusiastic Energizers

1. We can not direct the wind but we certainly can adjust our sails in order to enjoy success.

2. Set your goals high and remember that obstacles are the things you see when you take your mind off of your goals.

3. Happiness depends on external things that "happen" to us. Joy is a deep quality that we choose in spite of what is happening to us.

4. We may at times lose momentum but we can not afford to lose hope.

5. To be successful in whatever we do we must first have a vision of ourselves as successful. Keep your vision alive from day to day.

Excerpts from *Motivational Moments for the Workplace:* an audio series of inspiring and empowering messages complied by Audrey LeGrand.

Chapter 7 - Ethics

A discussion on ethics has to be included as we continue to explore our job jailbreak. Business ethics center on employee rights and we often see this displayed or acted out in specific behaviors exhibited by the employees of a company.

We define ethics as those guiding principles that help us decide between what is right and what is wrong. It is how these behaviors are seen and their implications that indicate what individuals will do when faced with a moral or ethical dilemma in the business world. For example, employees expect personal information to be confidential but it leaks out, that says something about the organization and its environment with respect to confidentiality.

Unfortunately, these guiding principles are not specific rules, rather established acceptable parameters in which we are to operate. In the last several years these guidelines have come under cross-examination and intense scrutiny. Major U.S. corporations, CEO's, Presidents, CFO's and even average employees have been cited as fostering an environment where questionable practices have been allowed to grow. We have Wall Street investors and dealmakers epitomizing the theme of greed as good or defense contractors gauging the government on contracts in which they supplied services or products at ridiculous prices.

While most industries are governed and regulated by federal, state and/or local laws, when we speak of ethics, we are referring to actions that go beyond what is required by the law. Just because an employee adheres to the law does not make their general practices and behavior ethical. An employee's activity may be legal, while their intent may be suspect.

For example, an interior designer inflates the price of home furnishings being sold to a wealthy client so their total sale will reach a particular dollar value, thereby giving the designer a larger commission ratio. The end result may be good for someone but the means are dishonest.

Bad choices are all around us and individuals make them every day. Most resumes are embellished by 63%. Our accomplishments are over-stated.

Your boss fudged the numbers on the departmental budget to ensure that more money was available for employee raises. Business ethnics often play out this way in corporate America every day.

Each individual must make a conscious decision every day about their actions and behaviors. Remember good ethics might best be summed up by asking what you would do even if no one was watching you or depending on you. Would you be happy with your actions at all times?

Chapter Review

Employing Ethics Everyday

1. Your moral compass must always point north during all of your business dealings

2. Make ethically correct decisions concerning your career at every turn in your career

3. Your actions/behaviors must never be called into question

4. Your walk must match your talk at all times

5. Remember everyone else might be doing it, but that doesn't make it right for you

Notes

Chapter 8 -Business Relationship

Relationship Rules

You will find the more work-based relationships you can successfully build will help propel your career and business endeavors forward. One of the top five skills for all professionals to have is the ability to work well on teams. That simply means how well others feel they get along with you.

The evidence of your ability to successfully connect with different people will be seen in how eager people are to help you succeed in your endeavors. If people are willing to help you, if people are trying to get on your team, or they are excited to hear the sound of your voice when you call with a request, you're in good shape. Continue to do what you have been doing to build sound and productive work-based relationships.

If you find yourself in constant battle with your co-workers, peers, or bosses you have to take a moment and examine how you are interacting with these people; not how other people react to you. It is how you approach and interact with others that must be called into question.

There will be certain difficult personality types that you will encounter at various times in the advancement of your career. In this chapter we examine 6 difficult personalities and some of the most successful techniques to handle these difficult people.

As you continue to pursue your ultimate career or profession, examine your interpersonal relationship skills with people. There are five basic people skills that all savvy professionals develop along the way in their careers. Dale Carnegie once said, "Your success depends on 85 % of your people skills and only 15% of your technical skills." The power of persuasion is the ability to play or participate well on teams in the corporate world using effective communication and interrelationship skills.

Five Relationship Rules

I. Give people your full attention when communicating with them

    a) eliminate distractions

    b) call people by their names

    c) give verbal and nonverbal cues that you are really listening to them.

2. Give respect to others to get respect from others

    a) R = reward-encourage others

    b) E = enthusiasm catches, show yours off

    c) S = service-help others

    d) P= partner-be a mentor or find a mentor

    e) E = etiquette-treat others right

    f) C = communicate effectively

    g) T = 'thank you' and 'please' go a long way

3. Develop a reputation for dependability

    a) return phone calls and email messages promptly

    b) when you make a promise or commitment, honor it

    c) don't promise what you can't deliver - under promise and over deliver

    d) respond to your customers, clients, employees and peers needs promptly

    e) the saying "your word is your bond" should be your hallmark.

4. Be willing to go the extra mile

    a) take on challenges others won't touch

    b) work long and hard to master something new- until you are willing to do something you have never done before, you will never learn anything new

5. Put yourself in the other person's shoes

   a) don't be so quick to judge without knowing all the facts

   b) unless asked, often keep your opinions to yourself

Everyone who comes across your path will **NOT** be a pleasant person. As you become more and more focused on your goals you will find that the individuals and resources you need to achieve these goals will come into your life. However, everyone may not be easy to deal with. Let's discuss how to handle difficult people, now.

Understand that less than 1% of the total working population is down right mean and evil. The rest fall into six easy to recognize and tolerable groups to manage. Let's identify these groups and outline effective ways to handle each personality type.

There are five fears that keep us from confronting people in our lives about their behavior towards us in personal settings, casual situations and professional circumstances. They are:

1. fear of injury - they'll hurt me

2. fear of failure - that didn't go well

3. fear of hurting their feelings - they didn't deserve that

4. fear of rejection - they'll never like me now

5. fear of financial insecurity - I'll lose my job for sure if I say that

As you review each personality type, identify individuals in your life who fit each description and how you have handled situations in the past. Then make a decision to never allow a particular type of person to control your professional career or personal life again.

The Angry Type

Angry Amy uses anger to manipulate, control, and irritate people around her. Subtle yet rude comments made one-on-one towards an individual or a group becomes the angry person's trademark. They are famous for biting sarcasm and a well-timed roll of the eyes. The angry person's passion in life is to make all of those who come in contact with them appear foolish.

Best way to handle this group

a) defuse the anger by listening to them and allowing the person to get the whole story out without interruptions

b) clarify the problem; get answers to who, what, when, where, why, and how

c) offer suggestions and alternative solutions

d) end the conversation on a positive note - people remember the last thing they hear

Example: Angry Amy is a customer service representative at a call center. Her demeanor with customers is unacceptable. After being reprimanded by her boss, she becomes angry and threatens the supervisor she feels was picking on her.

Using the techniques mentioned above how would you resolve this issue with Angry Amy?

_____

_____

_____

The Intimidating Type

Intimidating Ida is always in full throttle and fast forward confrontational mode. Her communication style is direct, pointed, and at or beyond the threshold of angry. Usually when people get wind the intimidator is coming, they run for cover. As quickly as the intimidator's tidal wave of intimidation comes, it will soon be over. You will often be left wondering what just ran you over at 95 miles per hour. Her pushy and aggressive behavior is her trademark.

Best way to handle this group

a) show a great deal of confidence when communicating with them

b) remain calm (list possible threats and responses in this section)

c) state your position and don't back down

d) don't give in to their demands

Example: Intimidating Ida is a mid-level supervisor who likes to yell at her employees and embarrass them in front of others. She tends to be very high strung and whenever things don't go her way she explodes. Intimidating Ida will sit at her desk and yell out the name of the employee she thinks has created an offense. She is often observed screaming up and down the hallway letting everyone within earshot know about the offense. Her employees cringe when Ida starts yelling. Morale is at an all time low and everyone wishes they had a job somewhere else. Based upon the above-mentioned techniques how would you resolve this situation with Intimidating Ida?

_____

_____

_____

The Whining Type

Whining Wendy feels helpless and overwhelmed by an unfair world. In her world, no one, and nothing will come close to measuring up to her self-imposed perfection standards. Whining Wendy is forever complaining about her problems to anyone who will listen. When you attempt to offer solutions to Whining Wendy, you become the enemy in her eyes and the whining escalates because she now has something new to whine about.

Best way to handle this group

a) take charge of the situation early on to keep the whining to a minimum

b) maintain a business-like approach

c) keep repeating the facts and alternatives

d) express no sympathy, show only empathy.

Example: Whining Wendy is forever complaining. In the summertime the office is too hot; in the wintertime the office is too cold. The chairs are uncomfortable, breaks are too short, the bathrooms are unclean, the food in the cafeteria is not good. Wendy just whines, whines and whines. Based upon the above-mentioned techniques, how would you go about handling Whining Wendy's concerns?

_____

_____

_____

The Often Mistaken Type

Often Mistaken Oscar is known to react and conform to the demands on his time by forgetting prior commitments and his previous decisions. Therefore, he often asks to be forgiven for making yet another mistake (or forgetting a meeting or important detail). He is famous for putting himself last and becoming a shrinking violet until the day he simply explodes over the least little thing.

Best way to handle this group

a) handle with extreme diplomacy

b) find a way to save their face and make you look bigger, better and brighter

c) never point out exactly where they are wrong

d) correct the situation and move on

Example: Often Mistaken Oscar is like the absent-minded professor. He forgets everything as soon as it is told to him. He keeps getting shifted from department to department because of his airheadedness, but it doesn't seem to help. He forgot to wear mandatory goggles in the machine shop area. When moved to the night shift, Oscar would forget to bring his keys to open the shop the next morning. He's a heck of a nice guy, but no one can trust what he says because his mind is always somewhere else. Using the above-mentioned techniques, how would you handle the situation with Often Mistaken Oscar?

_____

_____

_____

The Know-It-All Type

Know-It-All Kevin as his name implies, believes he knows it all, has seen it all, and done it all. Seldom in doubt of his answers or knowledge on a particular subject. Know-It-All Kevin has a very low tolerance level for correction from his peers and superiors, and none from his subordinates. To contradict him is to sign your own death warrant. This group is also known as the "I told you so" group. If his directions or advice are not followed to the letter of the law, Know-It-All Kevin speaks with the same grand authority concerning who is to blame, YOU!

Best way to handle this group

a) don't expect to win-compromise

b) decide what you can compromise on

c) don't get defensive-never take it personally

d) resolve issues quickly and move on

My co-worker Know-It-All Kevin knows everything or at least he thinks he does. No matter what has happened he has a story that will top yours. For every pain, he has a pain story that's more painful. No matter where on earth you've been, he's been somewhere better or had a better experience than you when he was there. Kevin's totally annoying. You want to run away when he walks in the room. Based upon the above mentioned techniques, how would you handle the situation with Know-It-All Kevin?

_____

_____

_____

The Verbally Abusive Type

Verbally Abusive Vince can be chugging along nice and calm, even silently until a communication encounter triggers his emotional nerve. His eyes widen, his facial expressions tighten, and his hair stands at attention on the back of his neck. His arms fold automatically across his chest and the moment his mouth opens his speech pattern becomes a series of blocked out, censored words that would make anyone embarrassed for the moment. And just as quickly as he exploded, Verbally Abusive Vince will storm out of sight.

Best way to handle this group

a) move quickly to stop this person

b) warn them first then cut them off

c) display a lot of self confidence

d) stand your ground, don't back down

Example: Verbally Abusive Vince, the general manager of a manufacturing plant, fancies himself a "verbal ninja" and thinks that he is comical. Our silent nickname for him is "worm-tongue." He's mean to everyone most of the time. He's not overt and loud. He's subtle and mean. Last week he told Charles in front of everyone that he was too fat and it was costing the company money in broken chairs. Verbally Abusive Vince laughed at George's report and insulted him in front of everyone at the meeting. Darryl, who works directly with him reacts in a way that is passive aggressive, lest be laughed at in front of everyone. Vince is not only verbally abusive but his continual put-downs of everyone are emotionally abusive as well. Based upon the above mentioned techniques how would you resolve the situation with Verbally Abusive Vince and his co-workers?

_____

_____

_____

Chapter Review

Respectful & Reciprocal Relationships

1. Use the platinum rule – treat others the way they would like to be treated, not the way we want to treat them, because that's easier for us.

2. Respect the rights and wishes of others to be different from us.

3. Learn the characteristics of all the difficult personality types.

4. Concentrate on learning to work well with at least one of the very difficult personality types in the workplace.

Eight Ways to Recession Proof Your Career

1. Ensure your employability

    a) keep your skills sharp and your knowledge up to date

    b) get the required credentials to be proficient in your area of interest

    c) know the minimum financial investment required for your transition

    d) diversify - don't put all your eggs in one basket

2. Have four streams of income

    a) have a day/night job for your main source of income

    b) get paid for your creativity

    c) have some investments

    d) receive income from seed sowing

3. Establish personal and professional goals

    a) create a written goals plan

    b) learn to embrace change

    c) identify your key skills

    d) do something every day toward your goals

4. Master the critical skills that all professionals need

    a) excellent verbal communication skills

    b) writing skills with good grammar

    c) listening skills - master this and double your communication effectiveness

    d) critical thinking-analytical problem solving skills

    e) become a team player and work well on your own

5. Build strong professional relationships

a) make connections outside your workplace

b) develop relationships with people in different departments within your current organization

c) be friendly, genuine, dependable and honest in all your endeavors

6. Maintain high visibility

a) figure out how to stand out/stand above the crowd

b) volunteer for hard, unwanted or high visibility projects and succeed at them

7. Be accountable

a) take responsibility for all your actions

b) admit your mistakes and find solutions

c) own up to your errors and gain respect

d) blame others and you'll destroy the trust they have in you

e) make excuses and you'll destroy your own credibility

8. Fortify your finances

a) know that you are not owned by debt- create a plan to eliminate your debt; this will take time, be patient

b) if you lose a client or your current job, have enough money in the bank to tide you over until you replace the client or the job

c) stop making ridiculous sacrifices just to maintain your current standard of living

By now, I sincerely hope you have discovered your natural abilities and are beginning to formulate a long-term career strategy that includes securing the type of employment your heart desires.

Remember this can be done in 3 different ways:

1. Reorganizing the job responsibilities you currently have to fulfill your career needs

2. Securing new employment to meet your long-term heart desires

3. Building a plan of action to pursue the business endeavors you long for

Time is of the essence now. Every day is another opportunity to achieve at least one small, yet incredible accomplishment toward your larger goal. It is imperative that you create a written plan each day. The plan must include the action steps you need to take to achieve your daily goals, then weekly, monthly, quarterly and yearly goals.

Remember, until you write your goals down and the steps necessary to reach these goals, you are just wishing or dreaming for something to happen. Once these action steps are written down and reviewed on a daily basis you will visibly be able to see your progress.

S.M.A.R.T. goals are designed in this manner:

1. **S**pecific - be as detailed as you can get. Draw a *small* picture, not a large one.

2. **M**easurable - how will you know when you have reached this goal? What is your yardstick or assessment tool?

3. **A**ctions - what must you physically do to make this specific goal happen?

4. **R**ealistic - is this going to happen or do you need to do something else first?

5. **T**imeframe - when will you start? Give a completion date when you will have this specific goal completed. *Once again,* give a date. These dates can be changed as you add action steps or change directions, but remember you must start somewhere.

Now you have a **S.M.A.R.T.** goal and you are using your time wisely.

S.M.A.R.T. GOAL SETTING

First Smart Goal to begin your release from Job Jail

Specific - _____

_____

Measurable - _____

_____

Actions - _____

_____

Realistic - _____

_____

Timeframe - _____

_____

Many goals will need to be identified and achieved between these two goals

Ultimate Smart Goal for your future career

Specific - _____

_____

Measurable - _____

_____

Actions - _____

_____

Realistic - _____

_____

Timeframe - _____

_____

More S.M.A.R.T. Worksheets can be found in the Appendix.

My wish for you is that you understand:

You only have a minute

only 60 seconds in it

forced upon you

you can't refuse it

you didn't see it

you didn't choose it,

However, it is up to you to use it

you must suffer if you lose it

give an account if you abuse it

it's just a tiny minute

but your, whole future is in it!!!

—Author Unknown

Get Out of Job Jail!

Special Credits

I want to acknowledge that the information contained in the first chapter on communication skills is a compilation of material I have been exposed to and trained on delivering over the past 25 years of my training career. This material is clearly a mixture of many different communication exercises and communication style dynamics, which have been blended together into one complete package for this book. The material has hopefully been presented in an easy to follow format for the reader.

Appendix

C.A.R.S Worksheets

S.M.A.R.T. Goal Setting Worksheets

Notes

Exercise: Create get up and go for your resume using the C.A.R.S. acronym.

Challenge + **A**ction + **R**esults + **S**cope = Career Accomplishment Statement for my resume.

C = Challenge

_____

_____

_____

A = Action

_____

_____

_____

_____

R = Results obtained

_____

_____

_____

S = Scope

_____

_____

_____

Career Accomplishment Statement

_____

_____

_____

Exercise: Create get up and go for your resume using the C.A.R.S. acronym.

Challenge + **A**ction + **R**esults + **S**cope = Career Accomplishment Statement for my resume.

C = Challenge

_____

_____

_____

A = Action

_____

_____

_____

_____

R = Results obtained

_____

_____

_____

S = Scope

_____

_____

_____

Career Accomplishment Statement

_____

_____

_____

Exercise: Create get up and go for your resume using the C.A.R.S. acronym.

Challenge + **A**ction + **R**esults + **S**cope = Career Accomplishment Statement for my resume.

C = Challenge

_____

_____

_____

A = Action

_____

_____

_____

_____

R = Results obtained

_____

_____

_____

S = Scope

_____

_____

_____

Career Accomplishment Statement

_____

_____

_____

S.M.A.R.T GOAL SETTING

First Smart Goal to begin your release from Job Jail

Specific - _____

_____

Measurable - _____

_____

Actions - _____

_____

Realistic - _____

_____

Timeframe - _____

_____

**Many goals will need to be identified and achieved
between these two goals**

Ultimate Smart Goal for your future career

Specific - _____

_____

Measurable - _____

_____

Actions - _____

_____

Realistic - _____

_____

Timeframe - _____

_____

S.M.A.R.T GOAL SETTING

First Smart Goal to begin your release from Job Jail

Specific - _____

_____

Measurable - _____

_____

Actions - _____

_____

Realistic - _____

_____

Timeframe - _____

_____

Many goals will need to be identified and achieved between these two goals

Ultimate Smart Goal for your future career

Specific - _____

_____

Measurable - _____

_____

Actions - _____

_____

Realistic - _____

_____

Timeframe - _____

_____

S.M.A.R.T GOAL SETTING

First Smart Goal to begin your release from Job Jail

Specific - _____

_____

Measurable - _____

_____

Actions - _____

_____

Realistic - _____

_____

Timeframe - _____

_____

**Many goals will need to be identified and achieved
between these two goals**

Ultimate Smart Goal for your future career

Specific - _____

_____

Measurable - _____

_____

Actions - _____

_____

Realistic - _____

_____

Timeframe - _____

_____

Notes